For David —T.L.B.

For Abbie, Sydney, and Brandon —D.L.D.

To Antonio and Giulio, and their colorful world —F.S.

Our deepest thanks to Sarah Davies, Rotem Moscovich, Heather Crowley, and Jamie Alloy. And special thanks to Daniel Mickus and David Schneider of 3M, as well as to Isabella Whitworth for her expertise in historic dyeing processes. And to Anthony Travis for his review of our manuscript. Any remaining errors are our own.

First Edition, October 2020
10 9 8 7 6 5 4 3 2 1
FAC-029191-20234
Printed in Malaysia

This book is set in Mrs Eaves/Fontspring
Designed by Jamie Alloy

Library of Congress Cataloging-in-Publication Control Number: 2019945904
ISBN 978-1-368-03284-1
Reinforced binding
Visit www.DisneyBooks.com

PERKIN'S Perfect PURPLE

How a Boy Created Color with Chemistry

By Tami Lewis Brown and Debbie Loren Dunn

Illustrated by Francesca Sanna

DISNEP · HYPERION

Los Angeles   New York

In 1838, Queen Victoria of England commanded,
*Make me a coronation crown of purple velvet,
and silver and gold,*

and diamonds,

and rubies,

and pearls.

The purest metals! insisted her goldsmith.

The largest diamonds! The reddest rubies! her jeweler said.

The fattest oysters with the most humongous pearls!
her diver declared.

Purple is tricky,

sulked her cloth maker.

Long ago, making purple was complicated. . . .

Hundreds of years before, in the ancient town of Tyre, Phoenicians harvested a certain snail. A marine mollusk named *Bolinus brandaris*.

They milked thousands—to release their foul-smelling liquid.

They cooked it with seawater and potash, then waited until it reeked.

But this secret recipe for
Tyrian purple was lost, and
so was the gorgeous shade.

So where could Queen Victoria's cap maker find perfectly purple velvet for her coronation crown?

Dyers used lichens, leaves, and lumps of wood,

bugs and berries, rocks and roots,

searching for a substitute for Tyrian purple.

But that color could fade unless . . .

they soaked the cloth in lime and URINE
to make the purple stay.

The cloth would STINK!
And it wouldn't really be the same as
the ancient shade. . . .

Yes.
Purple *was* tricky.

Until finally, years later, a boy named William Henry Perkin invented a new way to make purple.
Without snails.
Without bugs or berries.
And without urine.

This is how it happened.

William's father was a successful carpenter.

His brother, a proud architect.

Young William dreamed
of being an artist, a musician,
a photographer, or a botanist. . . .

William was interested
in everything!

When he was twelve, a friend showed him
experiments with crystals,

and he knew this was far more exciting
than any other subject.

He began to collect
glassware and equipment,
and set up a lab in his house,
in Shadwell, East London.

There he mixed and measured,
experimented and examined.

By age thirteen, he was studying at
the City of London School, near Cheapside.

Instead of eating lunch he listened to lectures on
crystals and calculations, matter and math.

Because William wanted to be a chemist.
To explore the elements that make our
world and to discover new formulas to
make the world better.

But his father said,

No!

Chemistry is nothing but trickery.
It's not a proud profession.
Be an architect, like your brother.

William begged.
His teachers pleaded.

And finally, his father gave in.

He paid for William to attend the new Royal College of Chemistry, a school supported by Prince Albert—husband of Queen Victoria herself.

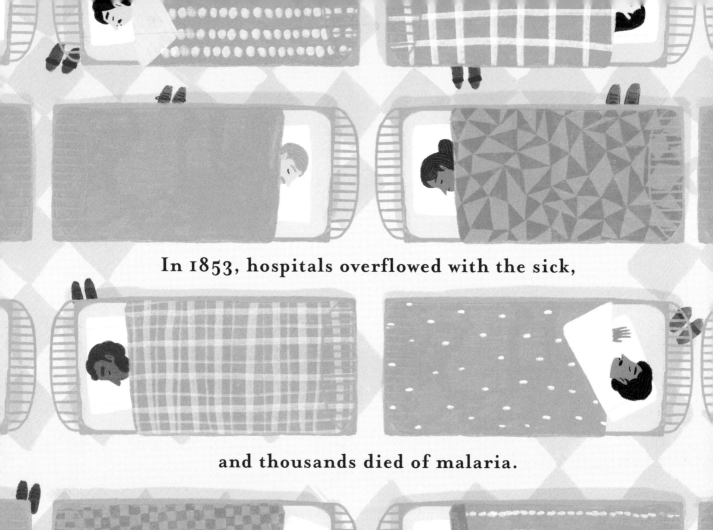

In 1853, hospitals overflowed with the sick,

and thousands died of malaria.

Quinine, the only known antidote, had to be
distilled from the bark of a small Peruvian tree.
Only the rich could afford this cure.

August Wilhelm von Hofmann, William's teacher at the Royal College, was an expert on coal tar—the messy leftover when coal was used for fuel.

Hofmann speculated that the natural building blocks of quinine were similar to the building blocks of coal tar. They had tons of coal tar.

Hofmann wondered, What if we use the tar to synthesize quinine? And he offered William a step-by-step formula for an experiment.

William was eager for this challenge.
Could he cure rich and poor with chemistry?

Twenty parts carbon,
two parts nitrogen,
twenty-four parts hydrogen,
two parts oxygen.

Could he make quinine from coal tar as Hofmann imagined?

Hofmann warned,
It might not work, for this is chemistry.

During his spring break, in 1856,
in the tiny lab on the top floor
of his house, William tried anyway.

MIX coal tar with a reacting liquid—
a cold orange-red substance,

WAIT for hours . . . upon hours,
YIELD: Useless red sludge.

Noting every step in his lab notebook,
William kept trying. . . .

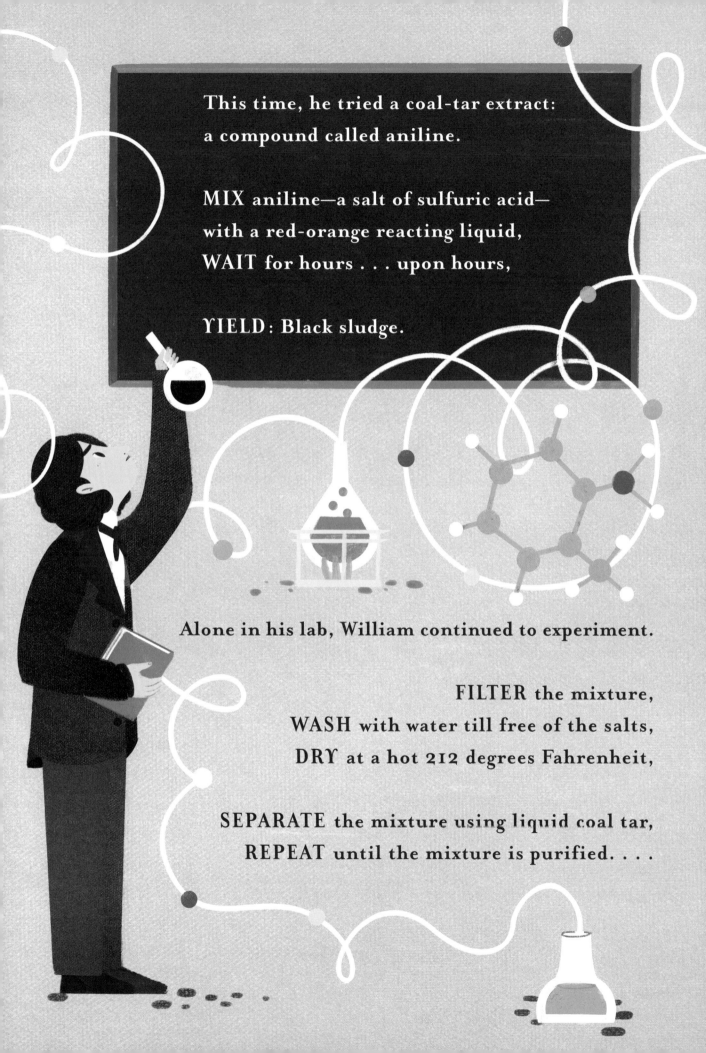

This time, he tried a coal-tar extract:
a compound called aniline.

MIX aniline—a salt of sulfuric acid—
with a red-orange reacting liquid,
WAIT for hours . . . upon hours,

YIELD: Black sludge.

Alone in his lab, William continued to experiment.

FILTER the mixture,
WASH with water till free of the salts,
DRY at a hot 212 degrees Fahrenheit,

SEPARATE the mixture using liquid coal tar,
REPEAT until the mixture is purified. . . .

But the experiment was a failure.

Quinine couldn't be made from coal tar.

Slowly and sadly, William prepared to clean his beakers;
he worried and wondered about the dark sludge.
His scientific training nagged and nudged—
perhaps he should go one step further.

Maybe . . .

a drop of pure alcohol to separate.
EVAPORATE the coal-tar liquid,
SEPARATE the mixture with alcohol, and
PURIFY it at 212 degrees Fahrenheit.

That was the moment William discovered that the black goo at the bottom was not just any black goo.

But what was it?
Examining further, he dipped a cloth into the solution. . . .

And the rag turned bright,

bold, rich, and royal

PUR

The tint of wealth!
The color of queens!

The pigment reserved
for bishops and
popes and kings.

PLE!

Perkin's vivid purple was concocted from
common sludge, not the milk of rare snails.

It wasn't the cure for malaria.
But could a color help people?
What good could his invention do?

William wasn't sure . . . but he knew his purple was important.

He could produce his purple time and time again,
by following his detailed lab notes. It didn't require
milking a thousand rare snails.

And Perkin's purple didn't STINK!

Best of all, William's purple would be
for all people, not just for nobility.

It was perfect!

So first to the market, in Piccadilly, he ran, to purchase white silk to dye samples.

Next, to the patent office, to secure his invention.

Then to find 400 pounds of coal . . . and 1000 gallons of water to get just one ounce.

But what an ounce! 500 drops of pure, perfect Perkin's purple!

Still, where Perkin saw purple,
others saw problems.

Dyers complained the color might
wash away or fade when it was exposed to light.

Professor Hofmann grumbled,

Purple is frivolous! Fashion isn't science!

But William knew—
one day acres of fabric
would be dipped in his dye.

And William's father knew—
he sold everything to invest in his son's endeavor.
And William's brother knew, as well—
he abandoned his architecture career to help.

They bought land to build a factory,
pooled their money, time, and labor.

And they called their company Perkin & Sons.

They tested Perkin's purple on different materials—
cotton, calico, wool, and paper. And William developed new ways
to keep the color stable on the cloth:
lightfast,
washfast, **permanently purple!**

Finally, William's invention was ready to unveil;
Oh là là. Perkin's purple matches my eyes,
Empress Eugenie of France cooed.
Queen Victoria declared, *Even better than my crown!*
Now I must have a purple gown!

So, Perkin & Sons did just that—
meters of silk and yards of velvet.
A bouquet of gowns for Eugenie,
as purple as fresh-plucked petals.
And a velvet dress for Victoria,
more purple than a setting sun.

Soon LONDON demanded, *Perkin's purple, please!*
PARIS couldn't get enough Mauve.
NEW YORK screamed for the Queen's Lilac.
From Europe to Asia, Africa to America,
everyone was adorned in purple
made by Perkin.
100% snail-free.

William's purple wasn't reserved for the rich and royal.
Purple for the people! Purple books and purple pencils,
purple socks and purple hats, purple gloves and purple boots.

Even Britain's postage stamps, "penny lilacs," were printed
with William's purple ink, and Queen Victoria's proud profile.

And William Perkin didn't stop there. . . .
His idea meant more than just one color.

William's discoveries uncovered
two thousand more shades,
a whole rainbow of colors.

His achievement led others to invent
in a new way: starting with proposals
and a hypothesis,
observing changes through each step,
and recording the results.

His systematic process helped scientists make chemicals to preserve canned foods for soldiers and to create original perfumes with scents that no nose had ever sniffed.

William's advances helped create medicine for immune disorders and chemotherapy, and cures for tuberculosis and cholera.

William's invention did save lives!

Perkin's purple set off
a chemical reaction—
a scientific revolution—
a brighter,
bolder,
healthier,
and happier tomorrow,
all thanks to a colorful chemist—
William Henry Perkin!

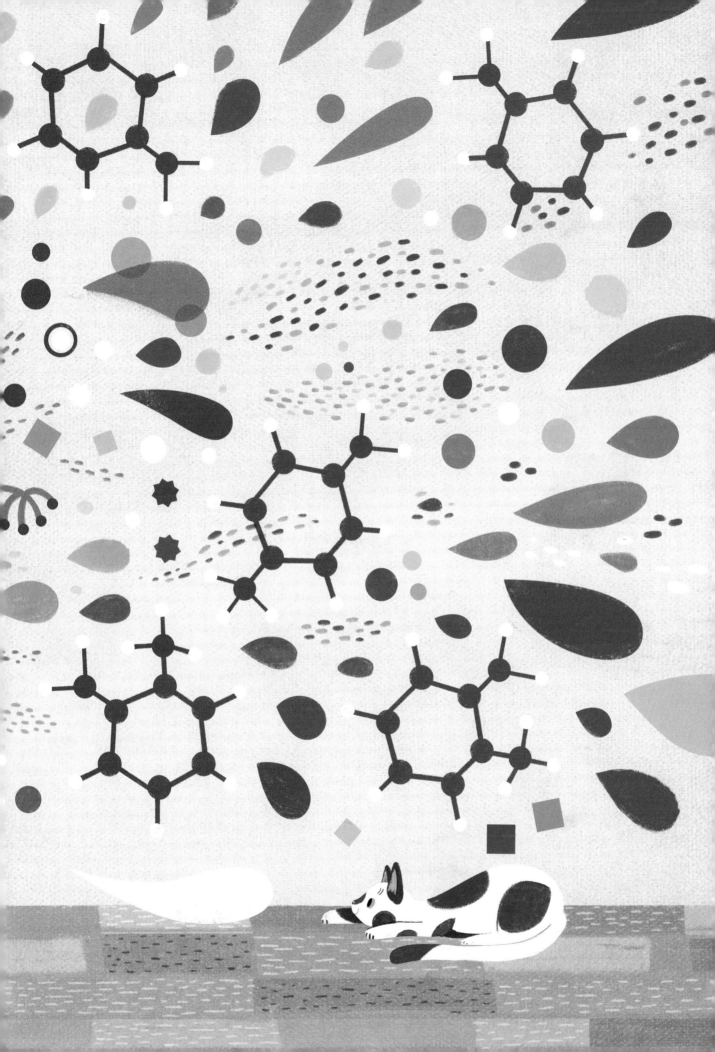

❧ *AUTHORS' NOTE* ❧

WHO WAS WILLIAM HENRY PERKIN?

William Henry Perkin, the last of seven children, was born on March 12, 1838, in Shadwell, at that time a poor neighborhood, in London's East End. William's father was a practical carpenter, but as an adult William visited his grandfather's former home in the north of England and made an amazing discovery. Thomas Perkin had hidden a small laboratory in his cellar, with a metal smelter and jars of curious materials. William's grandfather was a secret alchemist who'd attempted to transform ordinary metal into gold. No wonder his grandson went on to concoct vibrant purple dye and hundreds of other useful chemicals from sludgy waste!

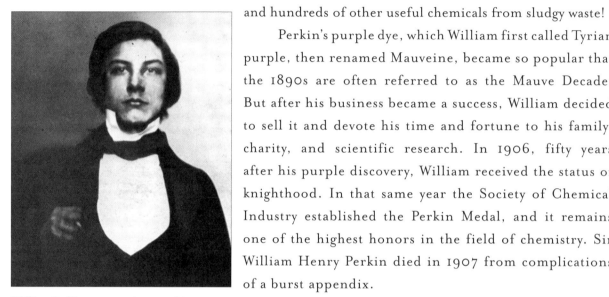

Perkin's purple dye, which William first called Tyrian purple, then renamed Mauveine, became so popular that the 1890s are often referred to as the Mauve Decade. But after his business became a success, William decided to sell it and devote his time and fortune to his family, charity, and scientific research. In 1906, fifty years after his purple discovery, William received the status of knighthood. In that same year the Society of Chemical Industry established the Perkin Medal, and it remains one of the highest honors in the field of chemistry. Sir William Henry Perkin died in 1907 from complications of a burst appendix.

William Perkin, age 14, photographic
self-portrait taken in 1852 (Science Photo Library)

WHAT IS COLOR, AND WHY IS IT SUCH A BIG DEAL?

For centuries colors have been markers of wealth and status. In England, Sumptuary Laws (up until the year 1603) strictly regulated that purple be worn only by close relatives of the royal family and religious leaders such as priests and bishops. Even after these Sumptuary Laws were relaxed, common people didn't wear purple because of its high cost. Yellow was the property of emperors in China during the Qing Dynasty. And in Tibet monks were known for their orange and red robes. Through the ages, most ordinary people wore drab fabrics colored by nature. Clothing ranged from natural browns to grays, with white cloth bleached by aged urine. Special garments could be dyed blue, rusty red, or yellow with roots, flowers, minerals, and other natural compounds, but William Perkin changed all of that.

Our ability to see color seems almost magical. Every object—from Queen Victoria's Perkin's purple dress to your yellow pencil or a red cherry—reflects light that invisibly vibrates in an up-and-down wave pattern. The cherry reflects light with the widest, slowest waves, between 620 and 750 nanometers, and our eyes see red. Perkin's purple silk reflects tight quick waves of light, from 380 to 450 nanometers. Without light there would be no color.

But the chemistry of William Perkin's invention was no magic. At the Royal College of Chemistry, Professor Hofmann proposed a theoretic formula to create synthetic quinine:

$$2(C_{10}H_{13}N) + 3O \rightarrow C_{20}H_{24}N_2O_2 + H_2O$$

Experimenting at home, teenaged William decided to use potassium dichromate, a dangerous orange salt, for the ingredient 3O. His recipe yielded dirty sludge rather than glistening white quinine. A lesser scientist would have washed his test tubes and given up. But at the Royal College of Chemistry, William had been trained to continue exploring until he solved problems for himself. So he persevered, swirling the sludge with alcohol to discover his purple masterpiece, the foundation for a new field of commercial organic chemistry.

A sample of Mauveine acetate dye probably prepared by William Henry Perkin around 1863–1864 (right) (Science Museum/Science & Society Picture Library)

HOW DID WILLIAM HENRY PERKIN'S INNOVATION CHANGE THE WORLD?

The impact of William Perkin's innovation is almost impossible to overstate. Perkin's purple led to several aniline dyes: Red, Black, Violet, and Green. But the color of our world is not the only thing William changed. The dyes that followed from Perkin's discovery allowed medical researchers to stain invisible bacteria and microbes, leading to cures for tuberculosis, cholera, and even anthrax. Methods he and others developed for changing the molecular structure of organic compounds, a process known as "Perkin's Synthesis," yielded synthetic smells and tastes that never existed before. Our world looks, smells, tastes, and feels different because of William Perkin.

Perhaps Perkin's greatest achievement was his central role in the "invention of the method of invention," the system of scientific exploration described by British philosopher Alfred North Whitehead. Rather than relying on good fortune, Perkin and other nineteenth-century colleagues began their scientific quests with a proposal—a hypothesis. Then, instead of combining random ingredients, Perkin intentionally and methodically worked a step at a time, making one change and then observing and recording each result and revising the hypothesis, as necessary. His painstaking approach was slow. It required patience and a tolerance for failure. But when Perkin's experiments succeeded, he knew why and he could repeat his success, again and again. In this way, Perkin and his peers not only invented scores of products; they reinvented the study of science and technology, our way of life today, and the world we will live in tomorrow.

Gram staining (Shutterstock)

WHAT IS THE SCIENTIFIC METHOD?

The scientific method is a methodical process for performing scientific experiments:

1. Identify a problem or make an observation.

2. Perform research.

3. Form a hypothesis (a prediction of the outcome of your experiment).

4. Perform the experiment.

5. Analyze the results and draw a conclusion.

6. Revise your hypothesis, if necessary, and experiment again.

7. Share your findings.

OTHER RESOURCES FOR COLORFUL KIDS:

To learn more about how kids (like William Perkin) can be great scientists, check out:

Beaty, Andrea. *Ada Twist, Scientist*. New York: Abrams Books for Young Readers, 2016.

Be inspired by the life of another great scientist by reading:

Berne, Jennifer; illustrated by Vladimir Radunsky. *On a Beam of Light: A Story of Albert Einstein*. San Francisco: Chronicle Books, 2013.

Queen Victoria inspired more than one invention. Learn about her bathing machine in:

Whelan, Gloria; illustrated by Nancy Carpenter. *Queen Victoria's Bathing Machine*. London: Simon & Schuster Books for Young Readers, 2014.

And colorful innovations continue today! Read all about it in:

Barton, Chris; illustrated by Tony Persiani. *The Day-Glo Brothers: The True Story of Bob and Joe Switzer's Bright Ideas and Brand-New Colors*. Watertown, Mass.: Charlesbridge, 2009.

Excellent resources written for adults about William Perkin, color theory, and history include:

Albers, Josef. *Interaction of Color*. New Haven: Yale University Press, 1963. Reissued 2013.

Blaszczyk, Regina Lee. *The Color Revolution*. Cambridge, Mass.: The MIT Press, 2012.

Finlay, Victoria. *Color: A Natural History of the Palette*. New York: Random House, 2003.

Gage, John. *Color and Meaning: Art, Science, and Symbolism*. Berkeley, Calif.: University of California Press, 1999.

Garfield, Simon. *Mauve: How One Man Invented a Color That Changed the World*. New York: W. W. Norton & Company, 2001.

*Queen Victoria in Perkin's purple for Princess Vicky's wedding in 1858
(Royal Collection Trust/Her Majesty Queen Elizabeth II 2020)*

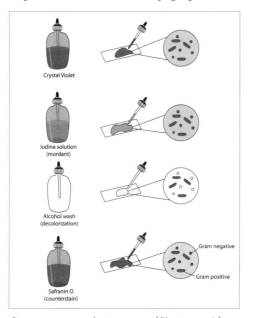

Gram staining technique steps (Shutterstock)

*Perkin & Sons Factory
(Science Museum/Science & Society Picture Library)*

*A few of the dozens of British stamps printed with
Perkin's purple ink and its descendants (Abbie Dunn)*

*Portrait of young Queen Victoria wearing her purple velvet
coronation crown (Royal Collection Trust/Her Majesty
Queen Elizabeth II 2020)*

PERFORM AN EXPERIMENT OF YOUR OWN:
DYEING CARNATIONS TO THE PERFECT SHADE

ONE: **Identify** a color you wish your flower to be.

TWO: **Prepare** by gathering the following items:

FOOD COLORING
A TALL CLEAR CONTAINER (VASE or CUP or even a BEAKER)
SCISSORS
WHITE CARNATION FLOWERS (or DAISIES)

THREE: **Predict** how much time will pass before the flower petals display the color chosen in step ONE.

FOUR: **Perform** the experiment:

Partially fill the container with water. Add several drops of food coloring to the water, enough to thoroughly color the water, and stir gently if necessary to distribute the color.

Arrange flowers in the container, with freshly cut stems submerged in the water.

FIVE: **Analyze** by observing the flowers at hourly intervals, recording the color of the petals at each check-in.

SIX: **Revise** if necessary, changing the color of food coloring, the stem length, or the amount of dye, and experiment again.

SEVEN: **Share** your dyed flower with a friend.